PERSONALITY BASED MARRIAGE

EXPERIENCE HEIGHTENED JOY, INTIMACY, SEX AND LOVE - IN LESS THAN AN HOUR (PRE-RELEASE EDITION)

JOEL & CASEY JOHNSON

Personality Based Marriage: Experience Heightened Joy, Intimacy, Sex and Love in about One Hour (Pre-release Edition)

Copyright © 2024 by Joel Johnson. All rights reserved.

ISBN: 979-8-9892414-1-5

This publication is designed to provide accurate and authoritative information in regard to the subject matter covered. It is sold with the understanding that neither the author nor the publisher is engaged in rendering legal, investment, accounting or other professional services. While the publisher and author have used their best efforts in preparing this book, they make no representations or warranties with respect to the accuracy or completeness of the contents of this book and specifically disclaim any implied warranties of merchantability or fitness for a particular purpose. No warranty may be created or extended by sales representatives or written sales materials. The advice and strategies contained herein may not be suitable for your situation. You should consult with a professional when appropriate. Neither the publisher nor the author shall be liable for any loss of profit or any other commercial damages, including but not limited to special, incidental, consequential, personal, or other damages.

CONTENTS

INTRODUCTION

"The definition of a genius is taking the complex and making it simple." — Albert Einstein

Adept thought-leaders take complex ideas and make them simple. This is what Casey and I (Joel) have sought to do with this short and straightforward book. Whether you're married, preparing for marriage, or desperate to rescue a relationship teetering toward divorce, we will teach you how to transform your marriage into everything you hoped it would be—in less than an hour.

A SHORT INTRODUCTION

Hello, my name is Joel. I'm so glad we're on this journey together! This is going to be fun!! My words will show up in regular font, as they are here.

Hi, it's so great to meet you! My name is Casey and my words in this book will be featured in bold font, like this.

Let's get started!

CHAPTER 1

MARRIAGE MATH

M ost married couples won't stay married for a lifetime—of those who do, many report experiencing less satisfaction and contentment with their marriage and spouse over time.[1] Unfortunately, this global phenomenon is a statistical fact. All the research proves it true.[2] But you don't need me (or science) to tell you that. You already know people experiencing this—feeling less satisfied and content in their marriage—and if you're married, statistically speaking, it's likely you feel the same way.

In the midst of this worldwide marriage crisis, how can you and your spouse beat the odds? Or more importantly, experience heightened joy, intimacy, communication, love and sex, with each passing year of your marriage? That's what this little book is all about.

MARRIAGE MATH

$$-1 + 5 = 0$$

For every one negative interaction a couple experiences together, it takes five positive interactions to counteract the effects.[3] — John Gottman, Ph.D.

In other words, your spouse needs to have at least six positive interactions with you—for each negative one—to generally feel good about your marriage. Yet, achieving that relationship ratio is easier said than done—especially when life-impacting decisions must be agreed upon by two very different individuals—with different needs, wants and personalities.

In the pages ahead, Casey and I (Joel) are going to lead you through a quick and easy exercise that will instantly increase the positive interactions in your marriage and lessen the negative ones. How do you and your spouse do this? We're glad you asked.

START HERE

It starts with gaining a clearer understanding of who you are and who your spouse is—how each of you think, make decisions, process information and act upon it. The way your spouse internally goes about doing all-of-the-above is radically different than what you may expect. And failing to understand these internal processes going on inside you and your spouse makes it impossible for both of you NOT to stumble into the same negative interactions again and again. Understanding your and your spouse's personalities is essential to beating the marriage-crisis odds and experiencing heightened levels of joy, intimacy, communication, love and sex with each passing year. The great news is that in the pages ahead we will show you how—in under an hour.

THE EXERCISE

You're just one exercise away from experiencing less negative interactions, and more positive ones so you can develop an increasingly healthy, fun and blessed marriage. Along the way, Joel and I (Casey) will share a few transparent stories of how we've incorporated this exercise into our marriage and how it transformed our union into a progressively growing head-over-heals, madly-in-love, joy-filled, sex-filled, fun-filled relationship over the past 20 years! The exercise you're about to engage in, is not new. In fact, you and your spouse may be familiar with it (or have taken a similar personality assessment). Yet, what you may never have done before is apply its results, specifically, to your marriage. Doing so is a total marital game changer! But before we jump into your personality

quiz (exercise), there's one brief item we must discuss if you're going to successfully apply the assessment's results to your relationship and experience a marriage that gets better-and-better—year-after-year!

Two Personalities are Better than One

Scripture reveals that every human has an unique personality, bestowed by a loving Creator:

> *"For you created my inmost being; you knit me together in my mother's womb."* (Psalm 139:13)

Or as the Message illuminates:

> *"Oh yes, you shaped me first inside, then out; you formed me in my mother's womb... body and soul."* (Psalm 139:13, 14 MSG)

According to the Bible, God not only formed your body in your mother's womb, He also formed your soul. Which means, before you were born, he gifted you with a personality-type all your own!

Though every human can learn new things, adapt, live out a healthier version of their personality—at the level of the soul—you cannot change the way God wired you (see Matthew 16:26, Mark 8:36). When you and your spouse understand the strengths and the weaknesses of the way each of you are wired, you can learn to complement one another, support each other in the way your souls were uniquely made.

And like I (Casey) learned marrying Joel, that in many ways it is actually because your spouse doesn't have the same personality as you do, God has afforded you the opportunity to experience a better marriage—a stronger functioning team—heightening levels of intimacy, communication, love and sex throughout the years of your relationship. So what exact type of unique personality do you and your spouse have? Let's find out.

IT'S GO TIME!

Please head to **16personalities.com** on an electronic device of your choosing and complete the FREE quiz (or if you'd prefer, you may purchase the Meyers-Briggs Type Indicator at **themyersbriggs.com**—either way you'll be fully equipped to move forward). After you receive your results, please write them in the blanks below. (For the purposes of this book, if you're using the **16personalities.com** assessment, we will only use the first 4 letters of your unique personality type—these first 4 letters parallel the 4 letters Meyers-Briggs uses.

When you've finished the quiz, please enter your and your spouse's personality type letters (and corresponding percentages) in the blanks on the next page.

YOUR PERSONALITY-TYPE LETTERS AND PERCENTAGES:

_____   _____   _____   _____

YOUR SPOUSE'S PERSONALITY TYPE LETTERS AND PERCENTAGES:

_____   _____   _____   _____

After you've taken the quiz and have your results, Joel and I (Casey) are going to unpack what the first four letters of your personality type are and learn what they tell us about you and your God-given personality. Additionally, please don't stress about this "test." There're no wrong answers. This assessment won't "define" you or put you in a personality "box." The purpose of the quiz is to help each of us discover how we are naturally wired and the unique personality God has given to us. As mentioned, this does not mean you can't learn new ways to think, act or make decisions. It simply reveals how you most naturally approach life. Transforming your marriage into everything you'd hoped it would be, starts now!

CHAPTER 2

EXTROVERTS &
INTROVERTS

EXTROVERT (E)

- Feels energized by the external world and social interactions

- Often enjoys socializing in large groups.

INTROVERT (I)

- Focuses their energy internally, on reflection, dreaming and understanding.

- Often enjoys socializing one-on-one or in smaller groups

ACCORDING TO THE ASSESSMENT...

Are you and/or your spouse an <u>Extrovert</u>?
If so, please fill in the appropriate blank(s) below.

(your E %) _____   (your spouse's E %) _____

If you both are extroverted, who has a higher percentage?

Are you and/or your spouse an <u>Introvert</u>?
If so, please fill in the appropriate blank(s) below.

(your I %) _____   (your spouse's I %) _____

If you both are introverted, who has a higher percentage?

Understanding your and your spouse's personalities is key to experiencing a better and better marriage year-after-year. Plus, it's fascinating (and also pretty fun)! So let's dive into the first characteristic of your personality test and see what the difference between an E (Extrovert) and an I (Introvert) is.

As shown above, Es are primarily focused on (and concerned with) the external world around them.

So all of you extroverts out there, like me (Casey)—you social butterflies—you're concerned with what's happening outside of you and around you.

We Introverts, or those extroverts near the introvert percentage line (like me, Joel), are more focused and concerned with the internal world. To us, surface level small-talk is boring and trite. We like to—be real—authentic—plumb the depths of wisdom with another old soul.

WHERE WE GET OUR ENERGY

Extroverts are oftentimes fueled by being around other people. That doesn't mean that you don't ever refresh yourself by being alone. It means that, generally, being with people energizes you. I (Casey) am an extrovert.

I (Joel) am technically an extrovert, but I'm close to the introvert line and much closer to it than Casey is. (And again, no one is 100% extroverted or introverted. We all fall somewhere between the two.) Introverts are fueled by being alone. Don't get me wrong. We like people. But we really enjoy fellowshipping one-on-one or in a small group. Generally, hanging out in a large group—for a long time—can be draining for us.

Most often, extroverts (like me, Casey) are also verbal processors. We "think as we speak." We tend to process out loud most of the time. Introverts, generally, are not verbal

**processors. They "think then they speak." They tend
to process internally.**

How we Communicate

If your spouse is an external processor, it may mean that
they tend to talk about what's on their mind. They process
out loud. And as I (Joel) have learned, a really great way to
love them is by listening. You create a highly positive interaction for your verbal processing spouse when you allow
them the space to process out loud and then ask clarifying
questions—resisting the temptation to "solve" their problem—but, instead bless them, by engaging in the conversation as they discover their own answers and resolutions.

As Casey briefly mentioned above, introverts often prefer to think before they express their thoughts, answers or
decisions out loud. They think first, process the information—formulate their opinion—then share.

Pro Tip:
- Extroverts often express themselves well verbally

- Introverts often express themselves well
  through writing.

So, if you're an extrovert fueled by being around people, and you married an introvert, who is more fueled by being alone, you might wonder why your introvert spouse didn't enjoy the large group function as much as you did—or why they were totally exhausted by the end—or why they couldn't bring themselves to go at all.

If you're an introvert and you married an extrovert you might find them communicating an issue to you to solve or a decision they need to make, and verbally vacillating between varying sides and outcomes. As an I (Introvert), you might find yourself experiencing thoughts like these about your E (Extrovert):

- Why are you telling me this?

- Have you had time to think about this?

- It sounds like you haven't fully defined the problem or what your opinion is yet.

- What is the outcome you'd like to see?

- Have you thought about this at all?

If the introvert is affected by the issue or plays a part in the decision making, they are likely to desire some time to internally process all that was communicated to them by their Extrovert. Introverts (and internal processors) often want to formulate their opinion before sharing it. They may even want to write a few things down.

Joel and I (Casey) process information very differently. I literally process, almost everything, out loud—in the shower, the car, everywhere. If I think it, I'm apt to say it. For Joel, not so much.

COMMUNICATION DISRUPTOR

If you are an extrovert, and you married an introvert, you might find them listening to you, but not responding, especially if the conversation is confrontative, combative or is going to lead to an argument, they will likely want a moment to internally process what you've said.

So, if you're like me (Casey), an extrovert, who verbally processes, I want to talk about a conflict or issue immediately. For example, if I perceive a shift in Joel and my "energy" or in one of our attitudes, I desire to talk about it—investigate it—and resolve it (if need be) as soon as possible.

In one of these past immediate and investigatory moments, I (Joel) was listening to Casey and all I could think to myself was "Okay, I don't want to respond in a wrong way here. I want to make sure every word that comes out of my mouth is right. I don't want to regret my response or add negative fuel to our current disruption in communication and potentially enter one of those negative interactions that I will then need five positive interactions to neutralize.

And I (Casey) was thinking to myself, "Wow, he is being so quiet and such a good listener right now...."

And I (Joel) was thinking... "I don't know if I have a prudent answer for that. I don't know how I feel about that right now. I'm not sure if I want to respond to that issue now—or potentially ever. (Smile.) I'm going to need a reasonable amount of time before I can formulate a cohesive opinion and then intelligently respond...."

Some of you reading this now, totally get what I'm saying. You don't want to end up saying something that you don't mean—or say it "wrong"—or say it in any way you're going to regret later. (We've all said things we wish we could take back, right?)

So, the more she's talking... the more I (Joel) feel like I don't have an appropriate answer or response for her. (Partly because her opinion seems to keep changing or she's communicated more issues besides the initial one.) I'm feeling pressured. Thinking if I don't answer her now, she is going to wonder why I'm not engaging with her and feel like there's a bigger—deeper—issue. I am also thinking, "If I do respond now, I'm probably going to say something inflammatory and I definitely don't want that...."

And I (Casey) at that point, continued to think, "He's being such a good listener right now."

And I (Joel) was thinking, "I'm feeling overwhelmed and exhausted right now."

As Joel listened and continued to be quiet, then I (Casey) began to wonder why Joel hadn't said anything yet." "Is he putting up walls?" I wondered, "Why is he doing this?"

Then I (Joel), seeing her facial expression become more inquisitive, start to think, "Oh no, she's starting to think I'm avoiding the issue, I'm upset or I am putting walls up.... This is about to get complicated.... I just need a few minutes to process all the passionate words, issues concerns and potentially life-altering decisions she has just presented me with...."

We now laugh at moments like this one—but they weren't funny then (at the start of our marriage)—they were entirely frustrating! The good news is that these highly negative interactions transformed into more positive ones, once we discovered each other's personality type. And now that you're recognizing each other's personality type, you and your spouse will surely experience the same.

When I learned that God had given Joel a much more introverted personality, who naturally processes internally, it helped me understand him more, and not take his silence as disinterest, disrespect or quiet defensiveness. He was truly engaged when I passionately expressed my concerns. He just wanted to formulate his opinion prior to his response, so he could share his thoughts as appropriately as possible. Through the personality assessment

(you just took), I learned he needed a little space and time to calm his emotions and process what I had shared. In a few minutes, he'd circle back and finish the conversation. Yet choosing to give him time to internally process, was not comfortable for me. It's not how I'm naturally wired, but it is how God wired Joel. And I wanted him to have the time and space—if it, ultimately, helped us come to a resolution—even if it wasn't as swiftly as I desired.

Through this assessment I (Joel) learned to verbally ask Casey if I could have time to think about the concern, issue or decision she was presenting (e.g. Casey, could I have a minute to think this over? May I sleep on this and we talk about it tomorrow? etc.)—instead of silently processing before her without saying a word.

Casey, that must have been really awkward for you back then?

I (Casey) love you so much, Joel... But, yes, it was...but just a little. (Wink.)

As an internal processor (and more introverted than Casey), I (Joel) am so grateful she allowed (and continues to allow) me space and time to process. But after I took the personality quiz, I discovered that Casey was (and is) an external processor and an extrovert. Because of this information, I now understood that her delaying the conversation was a sacrifice. Her desire to verbally process in the moment is the way God wired her. Until a conflict is resolved, it weighs more heavily—intellectually and emotionally—on her, than it does me. To accommodate me (and the way I'm naturally wired), she generously gave me space to think and process issues in the way that's most natural (and comfortable) for me.

While I appreciated Casey's accommodation to make this a more positive interaction for me, I (Joel), too, wanted her to have a more positive interaction in our communication and less of a negative one. I knew I needed to grow and see if I could accommodate her in the style of conflict resolution that was more natural for her—saving her from the negative drain that carrying unresolved conflict (especially with your spouse) can be. Yet, at the same time, I knew if I discussed the issue right away, I would likely express words that "didn't come out right" or that might be hurtful. I didn't want to do that either. In order to remedy this breakdown in communication, we created some relational "rules of engagement." Please allow me a moment to more fully color this in for you.

RULES OF ENGAGEMENT

If I (Joel) was going to engage in these conversations—meet Casey half-way—to more quickly resolve the conflicts we might experience in the future, I asked Casey for the freedom to say things "messy." That if I happened to express words that "didn't come out right"—or were hurtful—that Casey would seek to interpret what I said (and vice-versa) through a filter of best-intentions. If one of us did say something that was unclear, seemed unkind, untrue or disrespectful, we would give them the benefit of the doubt and then ask questions to help us gain clarity of the messy (or unclear) words that were spoken. We also agreed that whatever was said in these messy conversations, we would not hold against each other or use it as verbal ammunition in a future argument.

With these parameters, I felt safe enough to engage in these difficult discussions more quickly. This meant that Casey would experience less discomfort waiting on me to internally process before we resolved the conflict (a negative for her) and allowed me to feel comfortable to engage more quickly (also a positive for her).

Establishing these rules of engagement was hugely helpful to me (Joel), who was highly concerned with having the right words to say.

Once we understood our own and each other's personality better, it quickly helped both of us transform these negative interactions (in our communication) into more positive ones—for both of us. As you continue to learn more about both your and your spouse's personality, we know it will do the same for the both of you!

COMMUNICATION

Communication is so vital to experiencing a marriage that gets better and better over time. Like a gardenhose, when positive communication is "kinked" in a marriage, it automatically stops (or slows) the flow of relational intimacy.

And when a couple's closeness decreases, so does the joy, fun, love and sex shared between them.[4]

Gaining a greater understanding of your spouse's personality, will help you to better communicate with your spouse (and them with you). Better communication leads to deeper relational intimacy. And greater relational intimacy leads to all the most enjoyable interactions of your marriage!

QUESTIONS TO ASK YOUR SPOUSE

1. Who is an external processor?

2. Who is an internal processor?

3. What "rules of engagement" might help your communication be more positive and productive?

CHAPTER 3

SENSING & INTUITION

SENSING (S)

- Acts, presents and processes information in a sequential—step-by-step—order.

- Tends to describe the physical nature of things.

INTUITION (N)

- Focuses on the big picture. Easily sees opportunities and the value they could bring.

- Often speaks in stories and metaphors to describe things.

ACCORDING TO THE ASSESSMENT...

Are you and/or your spouse <u>Sensing</u>?
If so, please fill in the appropriate blank(s) below.

(your S %) _____   (your spouse's S %) _____

If you both are Ss, who has a higher percentage?

Are you and/or your spouse <u>iNtuition</u>?
If so, please fill in the appropriate blank(s) below.

(your N %) _____   (your spouse's N %) _____

If you both are Ns, who has a higher percentage?

Oh, this is getting good! Learning about you (and your spouse) is so fascinating and is laying the groundwork for your marriage to become better-and-better throughout the years. Let's look at the difference between a S (Sensing) and a N (iNtuitive).

S is for Sensing. I (Casey) am an S.

N is for iNtuition. I (Joel) am an N.

Needless to say, this has caused some marital turbulence throughout the years—especially in the beginning of our marriage. We'll shed greater light on these disruptive details a little later on in this chapter, in order to give you an example (a "case study") to see how you might successfully navigate these two personality letters in your marriage. But first, let's learn a little bit more about the Sensing and iNtuition personality types.

Speaking of details, those of us who are high "Sensors," love details and facts. I (Casey) know I do. They're very important and we oftentimes process information step-by-step (e.g. Step 1, 2, 3, 4, 5, 6, 7, 8, 9, 10). Sensing types are often naturally gifted at breaking down a big-picture vision into smaller—sequential—logical steps.

Speaking of big picture visions, those of us who are iNtuiton type, love to dream big. As I mentioned, I (Joel) am an N. If you're like me, an N, we don't naturally process or communicate information in smaller—sequential—logical steps. We process and communicate information in a broader way. We want people to see the big picture: describe what the vision is, what needs it will meet and the benefits it will bring to them and/or others. Unlike an S, the way we act upon, present and process information looks more like this: Step 1,

2—then we skip over all-the-other-less-important-details—9, 10. We process and describe the big picture snapshot of <u>why</u> we should do this, the vision and the benefit it will bring (for our marriage, kids, friends, finances, the world, etc.). They don't naturally see all the steps to accomplish the big picture vision. In fact, if you're like me (Joel), you're prone to lose motivation, enthusiasm and energy when you dig deep into the details; but seeing and sharing the big picture always is invigorating!

Pro Tip:

- iNtuitive personality types can naturally tell you WHY something should be done.

- Sensing personality types can naturally tell you HOW something should be done sequentially, in a step-by-step logical order.

Ns are attracted to big picture ideas and sweeping visions. They're interested in doing new and different things. When the logical step-by-step details need to be completed in order to finish the big picture vision, Ns often feel a desire to move on to a new—potentially bigger—vision. Generally, the Ss like me (Casey), who are most often actually working on the vision are saying, "Wait, I'm only at step 4. We haven't gotten to step 5, let alone step 10!"

Needless to say, if you're an N and you married an S (or vice versa) and you aren't aware of how they interpret information and communicate, it can cause some intense negative interactions.

Let me (Joel) give you an example from our marriage. When we first got married, I would freely communicate some of the big dreams I was having concerning our life and future. As I articulated the vision, unbeknownst to me, it was eliciting some very sequential—step-by-step—kind of thoughts within Casey.

Thoughts like these:

- We are going to be doing what?

- That is going to take years of work....

- The logistics alone are going to take hundreds of work hours....

- How are we actually going to accomplish all of this in our lifetime?!

These very logical and very linear thoughts ushered in waves of internal stress. This stress triggered her asking me very sequential—step-by-step—questions of how this was actually going to occur.

I (Joel) interpreted her stress filled disposition and her questioning as her communicating that she didn't believe in these dreams—which I was so vulnerably expressing—were possible! No, even worse, she might be inferring that she doesn't believe that I have the ability to achieve them at all. As she continued to riddle my visions with highly logical and reasonable questions, I couldn't help but feel a little mocked, hurt and angry.

After Casey and I (Joel) discovered that Casey was a S and I was a N, it enabled each of us to see how we could use our differences to turn the negative interactions, as I described above, into more positive and productive ones.

Let me (Joel) give you another example. In my last year of law school, Casey and I were traveling the nation speaking to teens in arenas and stadiums, wrote our first book and were expecting our first child, when I got this letter from Harvard Divinity School. When I received the correspondence asking me to attend a preview weekend at the school, it was a major surprise. I began to consider, pray and, of course, talk to Casey about it. (You can't keep something like that all to yourself right?!) I felt like I had to at least go and spend a weekend with them. So Casey and I flew out to Cambridge to spend a weekend at Harvard. Did I mention that she was quite pregnant at the time?

Cambridge? Honestly, it didn't seem good in the moment. But I (Casey) resisted the urge to say, "Joel, you're absolutely crazy!" Also, Joel had a Great Aunt who was thrilled at the opportunity, and offered to pay for our airfare and accommodations while we were there. That was so kind of her, and it allowed us to go without the expenses of it coming out of our household budget. Additionally, Joel offered to take me shopping when we arrived in Boston. (I have to hand it to him there. He was doing quite

a lot of preparation to make this experience a positive one for me.) So, of course, I agreed to go. Even so, I wasn't seeing how this was going to fit into our already busy lives.

After a weekend immersion at Harvard, Casey and I (Joel) had a better sense of what it would require and how this potential opportunity would, or would not, coalesce with all the other visions Casey and I were presently advancing. Casey and I took some time to talk through the pros and cons of walking into this potential opportunity during that season. Instead of me (Joel) feeling like she was doubting my dreams or ability, I chose to lean into her Sensing gift. Through it, she helped me to see things from a different perspective. We discussed the timing, the sacrifices it would require and the benefits it would afford us in the future.

The day Joel got the letter in the mail and he said he was interested, I (Casey) pretty much knew all the facts and details and many of the steps that it would take to enter this opportunity. But I also knew it was important to Joel and he's a dreamer and Perceiver (a personality we'll discuss in more detail in a later chapter.) I knew he would benefit from exploring this potential opportunity in person.

Casey was right. I (Joel) needed to explore this opportunity, or I would regret it in the future. As Casey and I discussed what it would actually take to accomplish this—the things we would gain, the very real sacrifices we would need to make, Casey asked me questions like these:

- What does this look like in practicality?

- Is this the best time and season to do this?

- Are we both ready (and able) to make the sacrifices this will require?

Her questions were asked in warm tones, there were no undertones of condescension in them, and as an N listening to an S, I was choosing to interpret her questioning as adding her God-given gift to this decision that would affect both of our lives. Her gift as a Sensor and my gift as an iNtuitive were powerful when we used them together to make the most strategic decision for our marriage and our family.

Ultimately, through Casey's wise questioning, prayer and exploration, I (Joel) came to the conclusion that entering that potential opportunity, in that season, was not best. Something, a very pregnant Casey, had already very much "sensed."

And I (Casey) think that was a really important lesson for Joel and me. Through a lot of painful disagreements prior to this one—and the personality assessment—we discovered that we processed information (and decision making) differently. Joel is incredible at seeing the big picture, perceiving creative opportunities and courageously entering into them.

Casey is really good at the details, creating sequential—step-by-step—systems and then effectively executing them. She's much more gifted in those areas than me (Joel).

In this scenario, I (Casey) held back my inclination to verbally analyze and breakdown this Ivy League idea—and not overwhelm Joel with all the little details. I was encouraging and let him explore and process the opportunity's pros and cons. We made the decision together and, ultimately, Joel and I both felt peaceful not moving in that direction. We haven't always done things well (and sometimes we still don't), but this was a scenario where we leveraged our gifts—how God naturally wired each of us—and came together to decide a very important potentially life-altering decision.

Two different perspectives—working together—are always better than one. And because we approached this decision, taking our personality differences into consideration, we avoided a massive negative interaction then—but also learned how to make more positive and productive ones together. This was a huge step toward transforming our marriage into everything we hoped it would be.

A decade later, after our trip to Harvard, I did get accepted to Harvard and studied psychology.

When spouses learn how each other are wired (their God-given personality) their unique perspectives and differences can become a couple's greatest strengths. This experience heightened our communication and relational intimacy; and these two positive interactions, set the foundation for us to experience progressively growing levels of joy, fun, sex and love. As you and your spouse get more acquainted with how God wired each of your personalities, you'll experience the same in your marriage as well!

There are so many good things to look forward to. Let's head into the next aspect of your and your spouse's personalities!

QUESTIONS TO ASK YOUR SPOUSE:

1. Who is more S?

2. Who is more of an N?

3. How can we use our personality differences to make more strategic decisions?

4. How can we use our personality differences to make more positive interactions?

CHAPTER 4
THINKER & FEELER

THINKER (T)

- Makes decisions by **"stepping back"** from the situation, and taking an objective view.

FEELER (F)

- Makes decisions by **"stepping into"** a situation and takes a subjective view.

ACCORDING TO THE ASSESSMENT...

Are you and/or your spouse a <u>Thinker</u>?
If so, please fill in the appropriate blank(s) below.

(your T %) _____ (your spouse's T %) _____
If you both are a Thinker, who has a higher percentage?

Are you and/or your spouse a <u>Feeler</u>?
If so, please fill in the appropriate blank(s) below.

(your F %) _____ (your spouse's F %) _____
If you both are a Feeler, who has a higher percentage?

Oh, snap! This is where most couples experience the most marital turbulence, but do not fear. This is also where couples experience the greatest breakthrough, transformation and learn to replace negative interactions with more positive ones. You are pages away from you and your spouse experiencing new levels of communication, relational intimacy, joy, fun, sex, and love with each passing year of your marriage!

I (Casey) am super high on the Feeler spectrum. Joel, finds himself near the middle of the Thinker-Feeler scale.

In our relationship, I (Joel) am more apt to make decisions as a Thinker.

Let's look at the differences between a T (Thinker) and a F (Feeler).

"Thinkers" are likely to:

1. Use their heads to make logical and reasonable decisions (considering how it best propels them or others toward a desired outcome).

2. Analyze the pros and cons methodically and consistently.

3. Express their thoughts directly and candidly.

4. Value truth over tact.

In our relationship, I (Casey) am more apt to make decisions as a Feeler.

"Feelers" are likely to:

1. **Use their heart to make values-based decisions (considering how it impacts people).**

2. **Are more apt to embrace ambiguity than Thinkers.**

3. **Often express their thoughts with courtesy, kindness and heart-felt empathy.**

4. **Value tact over fact.**

When you look at these four differences of how Thinkers and Feelers make decisions (above), you can see how it can set a couple up for major disagreements!

In many ways, a T's and a F's decision making process appears irreconcilable. If you're a T who has married an F (or vice versa), how should you proceed? God—who either made you more of a Thinker or Feeler—reveals the answer in Scripture:

> *"Instead, we will speak the **truth in love**, growing in every way more and more like Christ..."*
> (Ephesians 4:15 NLT).

When we learn to speak the logical, reasonable and objective truth (as a Thinker would)—in a way that those we are speaking to would best receive those words (as a Feeler would)—it leads us to speak, act and make decisions "more like Christ." Let me explain.

Jesus always spoke the truth in love. This required him to speak logically, reasonably and objectively (as a Thinker would)—in a way those he was speaking to would best receive his words (as a Feeler would). To love and guide those into an increasingly "rich and satisfying" life, Jesus had to exercise both the "Thinker" and "Feeler" portions of his personality (John 10:10 NLT). And to experience an increasingly "rich and satisfying" marriage, both spouses will need to learn to do the same.

When you and your spouse learn to lovingly speak the truth to each other, you will experience a heightening in your joy, relational closeness, communication, love and intimacy and will experience more positive and productive decision-making.

Pro Tip:
- Speaking in love isn't just about saying words filled with emotion, feeling or sappy sentiment. It's developing the skill of expressing what's truth in a way that the person you're speaking to will best receive it. (This can be easier said than done.)

Remember, speaking the truth in love, requires speaking the logical, reasonable objective truth (like a Thinker often naturally does) in a way that your spouse would best receive it (like a Feeler often naturally does). This necessitates that Thinkers learn to empathetically communicate to their more Feeler-type spouse and Feelers learn how to logically communicate with their more Thinker-type spouse. Learning how to speak the truth in love to your spouse will eliminate so many negative interactions and ensure waves of positive ones. So how do spouses accomplish this practically? Let me give you the play-by-play!

How to Speak the Truth in Love to Thinkers and Feelers

Instructions: Circle all the ways (below) you would prefer your spouse to communicate with you, especially when you have a big decision to make.

3 Ways for Thinkers to Speak the Truth in Love—to help you better communicate and make better decisions with your more—Feeler-type spouse.

1. Use Tact
Allow your Feeler to share their thoughts, resist passing judgment, no matter how irrational you may think their thoughts may be.

2. Talk to the heart.
- Verbally praise your spouse for the powerful perspective they bring to the table.

- Focus your attention on their body language and tone of voice to better understand how they're feeling as they talk.

- Give them ample time to process. Don't be in a hurry

to decide or criticize their thoughts and feelings before you really listen to what they're expressing.

- If you realize you're attempting to push them into thinking like you (a Thinker), apologize and stop.

- If your Feeler is having a hard time making a decision, you may gently remind them that most decisions rarely accommodate everyone or win the approval of all—and that's okay.

3. **Recognize the value of emotions in decision-making**.

Pro Tip:
- Mind-set Shift: God uses emotions and empathy in his decision making. God felt a compassionate love for humanity and sent Jesus to save us (John 3:16). He literally empathized with humanity by allowing Jesus to put himself "in our shoes" as a human. Is there any more loving (or better) way for humans to have received God's message of truth than through His Son coming as a human?

- Feelers can pick up on things that aren't always obvious, so use the gift to help you make better decisions. You may want to ask your spouse to make a list of any potential emotional outcomes for you and your kids (or any other pertinent individuals involved) on either side of your decision.

3 Ways for Feelers to Speak the Truth in Love—to help you communicate and make better decisions with your more Thinker-type spouse.

Instructions: Continue to circle all the ways (below) you would prefer your spouse to communicate with you, especially when you have a big decision to make.

1. **Use Facts**
   - Plan your argument ahead of time.

   - Win your Thinker over with logical arguments, data from experts and evidence.

   - And don't hesitate to argue for what's best for everyone, if needed. Thinkers often like it when you're clear and firm in your ideas (especially when they are founded in reason and logic).

2. **Talk to the head**
   - When you talk about your emotions do so in a clear logical way.

   - If possible, keep your points short and to the point.

- And if at any point in the conversation you find yourself assuming your Thinker does not have feelings, apologize—they do have feelings, but they don't often use them to make decisions.

3. **Recognize the value of logical reasoning in decision-making.**

- Thinkers see things at face value, so use it to your mutual advantage. For example, you can identify any hardcore yes/no solutions that you need to decide on and ask the Thinker to come up with the pros and cons or give a rapid-fire bullet point list of where potential outcomes might take you as a couple. Assign them any research tasks beforehand in order to gather relevant information that might contribute to making a good decision.

When both spouses work towards speaking the truth in love–developing the skill of expressing what's true in a way that your spouse best receives–that will eliminate negative interactions, and will make even the toughest decisions, discussions, or disagreements more positive. Adding this–speaking the truth and love technique–will make your communication so much more positive. And as you recall, the more positive your communication grows, the more relational intimacy you and your spouse will

experience, and it is relational intimacy that gives you access to heighten joy, fun, sex and love.

A QUESTION TO ASK YOUR SPOUSE

1. What is the number one thing (you circled above) that you would like me to incorporate into how I communicate with you? (Take turns asking each other.)

- Please feel free to bookmark this page and use the list above when you communicate—especially when you have big decisions to make as a couple.

WANT MORE?

Also, if you would like to hear more from Joel and Casey on the subject of Thinker & Feeler, please go to **joeljohnson.org/datenight (Date #2)**, and watch the video (and download the FREE "datenight" curriculum), or listen to the audio on **Messy Life Podcast (Season 2, Episode 15)** on your favorite podcast platform.

CHAPTER 5

JUDGING &
PERCEIVING

JUDGING (J)

- Approaches life in a structured, organized and carefully calibrated way, creating short-and-long-term plans to help them achieve their goals.

PERCEIVING (P)

- Are more flexible in making decisions and often absorb more information over a longer period of time.

- They adapt better to sudden change and can quickly adjust to make last minute decisions, if needed.

ACCORDING TO THE ASSESSMENT...

Are you and/or your spouse <u>Judging</u>?
If so, please fill in the appropriate blank(s) below.

(your J %) _____   (your spouse's J %) _____
If you both are Judging, who has a higher percentage?

Are you and/or your spouse <u>Perceiving</u>?
If so, please fill in the appropriate blank(s) below.

(your P %) _____   (your spouse's P %) _____

If you both are Perceiving, who has a higher percentage?

You're almost there! We are about to place the final piece into your (and your spouse's) personality puzzle! So you can experience more positive interactions and less negative ones and experience a marriage with heightening joy, meaningful conversation, relational intimacy, sex and love year after year. Let's look at the differences between a J (Judging) and a P (Perceiving).

Judging personality types like to use a planned approach in meeting a deadline in a scheduled orderly way. Perceiver personality types like to use a spontaneous approach in meeting a deadline with a flurry of energy and movement leading right up to that deadline.

If Js have 30 days to complete a project, they often find their inspiration—their motivation, their organization—day 1 through 15. They're planners, they love information and details. Js like to plan and execute early. It alleviates the stress they increasingly experience as they approach deadlines. Js generally don't perform as well under the pressure that last minute changes can cause.

Perceivers operate differently. They find their motivation, their energy, their inspiration as deadlines approach. If Perceivers have 30 days to complete a project, Ps often find their creative inspiration and motivation during day 15 through 30—and many have their best and most creative ideas emerge in the days, hours and minutes leading up to a deadline. Ps often perform well under the pressure of last minute changes.

As you might guess, when Judgers and Perceivers get married, they can often experience conflict.

J's may often view Ps as procrastinators who refuse to manage their time appropriately. Because Ps move into action closer to a deadline and don't mind making last minute changes, it can cause the Js they are working with, or married to, experience elevated levels of stress—often eliciting thoughts such as these:

- **Are they going to be ready in time?**

- **Will they be prepared?**

- **Do they have a plan?**

- **Why can't they seem to manage their time better?**

Ps are often just as perplexed about Js—often eliciting thoughts such as these:

- You need to relax. Stop "stressing." Loosen up. Live a little.

- Why can't you let go, go with the flow, be in the moment?

- Did you know there is such a thing as "over-planning"?

- It will all come together, at the right time, as it always does.

Js and Ps have two different ways of approaching tasks, deadlines and life. Whatever your spouse's personality type, remember, God wired them this way. It is a part of their personality—psychology—soul. If you're a J married to a P, or P married to a J, you can choose to look at your spouse's approach to life as a negative, or instead, see to make your different personality approaches more positive for you as a couple.

TURNING A NEGATIVE INTO A POSITIVE

I (Casey) am a J. I naturally like to plan things.

I (Joel) am a P and I more naturally live in the moment.

No doubt Casey and I (Joel) have experienced some friction in this area and we've had to learn to navigate our personality differences.

As I (Casey) just mentioned, I am very much a planner and so I've had to learn to leave more room for spontaneity in our lives. This shift has helped to foster more positive interactions between Joel and me.

I (Casey) have had to learn that one cannot control everything (especially outcomes) and that is okay and normal. So I will plan as much as possible and project that we are going to leave 20% up to spontaneous living. For me, planning helps me know what to expect next. When we have a plan, I feel less stress and that helps me relax—have more fun—so that when moments of spontaneity arise, I am open to fully engaging in them.

And I (Joel), on the other hand, have had to recognize that Casey is going to plan everything she can (that is her approach to vacations, finances, kids, schedules, work and life). Once I discovered that Casey was wired—by God—to plan ahead, I could see that many of the ways that I approach life as a P bring her additional stress and anxiety (a real negative for her). In order to help eliminate these negative experiences for her, and make doing life with me a more positive experience, one of the actions that has helped provide more peace for her, and for me too, is gathering at the start of each month to discuss our schedules and make plans for the months ahead. Even though it stresses me out when things feel over-planned, rigid or controlled, I do like having a plan. It's just that my plans aren't ever going to be as detailed as Casey's.

Now it's your turn to analyze your marriage through the lens of how you, approach life either as a J or P. Choose a past or present marital interaction and see if you can better understand it in terms of J type and P type personalities. (Apply what you've learned about better conversation, relational intimacy, and speaking the truth in love, to your discussion.) Follow the list of questions that we have prepared for you; they will help guide you through the conversation.

Pro tip:

If a "case study"—one of Casey and my stories—of learning to navigate our Judging and Perceiving personalities would be helpful, please go to **joeljohnson.org/datenight (Date #3)**, and watch the FREE video (and download the FREE "datenight" curriculum) or listen to the audio on **Messy Life Podcast (Season 2, Episode 16)** on your favorite podcast platform.

J & P Questions to Ask your Spouse

1. Who would you say is the "planner" between the two of us?

2. Who would you say is the more "flexible" between the two of us?

3. What strengths do each of our—more J-ish or P-ish—personality traits add to our marriage and/or family? (Mention one or more past instances where they have been a strength.)

4. Do you recall a time where we used our unique—more J-ish or P-ish—personality traits together and it made that experience we shared better?

5. Do you recall a time where our—more J-ish or P-ish—personality traits (and perspectives) may have caused marital turbulence or conflict?

6. Knowing what we now know about ourselves, and each other, how could we have used this knowledge or our—more J-ish or P-ish—personality traits to have avoided the conflict or to have, at least, brought about a resolution more rapidly?

CHAPTER 6

MORE JOY, INTIMACY, SEX AND LOVE

W hether you're married, preparing to be married or desperate to rescue the relationship you're in—by engaging with *Personality Based Marriage*—you've taken a big brave step toward transforming your marriage into everything you hoped it would be. You've gained a greater understanding of your and your spouse's God-given personality and, thus, removed a major obstacle to experiencing heightened joy, intimacy, communication, love and sex with each passing year of your relationship.

Remember, communication is vital to experiencing a relationship that gets better and better over time. Like the gardenhose illustration I (Casey) shared earlier—when positive communication is "kinked" in a marriage, it automatically stops (or slows) the flow of relational intimacy. And when a couple's closeness decreases, so does the joy, fun, love and sex shared between them.

To help foster your relational intimacy—expedite you experiencing all the best interactions of marriage—Casey and I (Joel) have prepared a list of questions and a prayer (below) that will not only increase the flow of positive communication, but also apply what you've learned throughout the book.

In addition, if you and your spouse have a question or would find it helpful to talk (Zoom) with Joel or me (Casey), you may set up a FREE 10-minute appointment or schedule a 50 minute coaching session at <u>www.whole hearted.university/coaching</u> or scan the QR code below.

Bonus Questions for your Spouse

Instructions: Start with question 1. Read the question to your spouse. After listening to your spouse's response, then respond with your own answer. Then move on to question 2. Repeat until you have exhausted the list below.

Please relax and have fun with this.

Now who's going to go first?

1. What is something you learned about your personality?

2. What is something you learned about my personality?

3. What aspects of your personality do you feel benefit our marriage and family?

4. What aspects of my personality do you feel benefit our marriage and family?

5. In which personality quadrant(s) — I vs. E, S vs. N, T vs. F, or J vs. P — do you feel we experience the most harmony in our relationship?

6. In which personality quadrant(s) — I vs. E, S vs. N, T vs. F, or J vs. P — do you feel we experience the most friction in our relationship? How do you think we could experience less friction?

7. What can I do to help us experience less friction in our relationship?

8. In what new ways might we use the strengths found in our personalities to help our marriage and family ("team") win?

A Prayer for Your Marriage

God is incredibly invested in your life and marriage. God sent Jesus to give us "more and better life than they ever dreamed of" (John 10:10 MSG). Asking God to enter your marriage and relationship is one of the most positive and productive things you could ever do. We have included the following prayer as a guide. Please take a minute to pray this prayer over each other and your relationship.

Father, I invite you into our marriage. Jesus, I invite you into our relationship. Holy Spirit, I welcome you into our union. We have experienced highs and lows, joy and pain, victories and disappointments. I ask you to enter my life and our marriage in a new way. Restore me. Restore _____ (your spouse's name). Restore our marriage.

Give me life better than I ever dreamed of. Give _____ (your spouse's name) life better than _____ (she/he) ever dreamed of. Give our marriage new life. Let it be better than we ever dreamed it could be. God, give me the grace, teach-

ability and humility I need to love _____
(your spouse's name) the way _____ (she/he) needs
to be. In Jesus' name. Amen.

YOUR NEXT STEP

THE WHOLEHEARTED JOURNEY BOOK & *WHOLEHEART-ED UNIVERSITY*.

WHOLEHEARTED UNIVERSITY is a 9-session experience (for small groups or individuals) that also includes:

- Live Classes (in-person or online)

- Workbook

- Digital & Audio Book

- Community Support

- Films and more

LEARN MORE @ www.wholehearted.university

1. Thorsten, K., & Gerrit, B. (2009). Did Unilateral Divorce Laws Raise Divorce Rates in Western Europe? *Journal of Marriage and Family*, *71*(3), 592-607.

2. Strizzi, J. M., Ciprić, A., Sander, S., & Hald, G. M. (2021). Divorce is stressful, but how stressful? Perceived stress among recently divorced Danes. *Journal of Divorce & Remarriage*, *62*(4), 295-311.

3. Gottman, J. M. (2014). What predicts divorce?: The relationship between marital processes and marital outcomes. Psychology Press.

4. Markman, H. J., Rhoades, G. K., Stanley, S. M., Ragan, E. P., & Whitton, S. W. (2010). The premarital communication roots of marital distress and divorce: the first five years of marriage. *Journal of family psychology*, *24*(3), 289.

NOTES

These pages are for you to write upon. Write down your story, your thoughts and the words God may speak to you. Whenever you write, I'd encourage you to also jot down the date, time and your location. In the years to come, this section will serve as a powerful reminder (and document) of what God did for you throughout this book and how far you've come since first reading this pithy and practical work, entitled, *Personality Based Marriage.* (We left these pages blank to give you the creative space to not only write, but to draw or sketch as well.)

Made in the USA
Columbia, SC
17 June 2024

36429016R00052